Sanctification of the Sabbath

Sanctification of the Sabbath

The Permanent Obligation to
Observe the Sabbath or Lord's Day

Robert Haldane

Reformation Heritage Books
Grand Rapids, Michigan

Sanctification of the Sabbath
© 2022 by Reformation Heritage Books

All rights reserved. No part of this book may be used or reproduced in any manner whatsoever without written permission except in the case of brief quotations embodied in critical articles and reviews. Direct your requests to the publisher at the following addresses:

Reformation Heritage Books
3070 29th St. SE, Grand Rapids, MI 49512
616-977-0889
orders@heritagebooks.org
www.heritagebooks.org

Scripture taken from the New King James Version®. Copyright © 1982 by Thomas Nelson. Used by permission. All rights reserved.

Printed in the United States of America
22 23 24 25 26 27/10 9 8 7 6 5 4 3 2 1

Library of Congress Cataloging-in-Publication Data

Names: Haldane, Robert, 1764-1842, author.
Title: Sanctification of the Sabbath : the permanent obligation to observe the Sabbath or Lord's day / Robert Haldane.
Description: Grand Rapids, Michigan : Reformation Heritage Books, [2022] | Includes bibliographical references.
Identifiers: LCCN 2021036454 (print) | LCCN 2021036455 (ebook) | ISBN 9781601789068 (paperback) | ISBN 9781601789075 (epub)
Subjects: LCSH: Sabbath. | Sunday.
Classification: LCC BV130 .H28 2022 (print) | LCC BV130 (ebook) | DDC 296.4/1—dc23
LC record available at https://lccn.loc.gov/2021036454
LC ebook record available at https://lccn.loc.gov/2021036455

For additional Reformed literature, request a free book list from Reformation Heritage Books at the above regular or email address.

Contents

Preface vii

Introduction 1

1. The Sabbath Anterior to the Mosaic
   Dispensation 5
2. The Sabbath Binding Alike under the Jewish
   and Christian Dispensations 11
3. The Manner of the Promulgation
   of the Decalogue 13
4. The Manner of the Preservation of the
   Decalogue and the Lessons Thereby Taught 15
5. Proof of the Permanence of the Fourth
   Commandment Derived from the
   Foregoing Statements 25
6. Internal Evidence Shows That the Fourth
   Commandment Is of Universal Obligation 29
7. Objections to the Permanent Obligation of
   the Sabbath Considered 33

8. The Observance of the Sabbath under the Christian Dispensation Is Fully Recognized by the Prophets 45

9. The Change from the Last to the First Day of the Week Has Not Invalidated the Obligation of the Sabbath 51

Conclusion 73

Preface

One biographer wrote astutely of Robert Haldane that he "was what the years had made him; the years, his heritage, and the grace of God."[1] Robert Haldane was born in 1764 to a noble family in Overton, Scotland, although his parents would die before he turned ten. Robert was educated under the supervision of relatives in Scotland until in 1779 he joined the Royal Navy. He lived an exciting life of service until, soon after attaining his majority, he married eighteen-year-old Katherine Cochrane Oswald and stepped into the role of elder son and heir to his father's noble lineage (and wealth).

Around 1795, Robert's brother, James, experienced a powerful conversion. James's newfound faith, along with the influence of pastor David Bogue in Gosport, would

---

1. Joe Ridholls, *Spark of Grace: The Story of the Haldane Revival* (Pool, Redruth, Cornwall: self-published, 1978), chap. 2, https://archive.org/details/SparkOfGrace.

prove deeply influential in Robert's own conversion.[2] Their warm, evangelical faith became known and spread abroad in ways that can still be seen today.

An Evangelical Leader

Robert soon directed his enthusiasm toward missions. He devoted significant amounts of his own fortune toward several missionary endeavors. He helped fund the Society for Propagating the Gospel at Home, training courses for future ministers, and the printing of tracts and Bibles for public distribution, and he helped organize a building fund to accommodate larger crowds to hear the preaching of God's Word.[3] He went on to fund the establishment of a seminary, the erection of

---

2. For more on the younger James Haldane, see Alexander Haldane, *The Lives of Robert and James Haldane* (Carlisle, Pa.: Banner of Truth Trust, 1990); Dudley Reeves, "James Haldane: The Making of a Christian," Banner of Truth, August 13, 2019, https://bannerof truth.org/us/resources/articles/2019/james-haldane-making-of-a -christian. James was a solid theologian in his own right. See, for example, James Alexander Haldane, *An Exposition of the Epistle to the Galatians: Showing That the Present Divisions among Christians Originate in Blending the Ordinances of the Old and New Covenants* (Springfield, Mo.: Particular Baptist Press, 2002), http://archive.org /details/anexpositionepi00haldgoog.

3. D. W. Lovegrove, "Robert Haldane," in *Dictionary of Scottish Church History and Theology*, ed. Nigel Cameron (Downers Grove, Ill.: InterVarsity Press, 1993), 386; Haldane, *Lives of Robert and James Haldane*, chap. 6.

tabernacles in six Scottish cities, the operation of Sunday schools, and the ongoing publication of Bibles.

But Haldane was not happy to let the hands-on ministry be left to his seminarians. He was an avid open-air preacher who preached with such vigor that he often injured his throat and had to sit out to rest. This nobleman traded in his worldly possessions and status for the life of a fool (1 Cor. 1:23). But he loved it, and God blessed it.

In 1816, Haldane and his wife left to visit the Continent for a few months, not knowing that God would have him stay on the mainland for three years. Those three years would prove to be immensely impactful, both on Haldane and for the kingdom.

Though it was not his plan, Haldane was persuaded to remain in Geneva, much like another foreigner, John Calvin, was persuaded nearly three hundred years earlier. In God's providence, Haldane met a young divinity student, and their relationship blossomed. The young man must have been quite impressed because the following day he returned with a friend, Charles Rieu. Haldane later wrote of these two students, "I questioned them about their personal hope of salvation, and the foundation of that hope. Had they been trained in the schools of Socrates or Plato, and enjoyed no other means of instruction, they could scarcely have been more ignorant of the doctrines of the Gospel."[4] Haldane had found his new ministry field.[5]

These young ministerial students were hooked, and many came to meet with Haldane at all hours of the day. He eventually started regular meetings, thrice weekly for two hours in the evening, in which the Bible and theology would be taught to any who would come. The divinity students loved it. One student said of Haldane, "Here is a man who knows the Bible like Calvin!"[6] And know the Bible he did. Haldane would regularly take twenty or thirty students and sit around a long table, on which were laid Bibles in French, English, and German, plus the original Greek and Hebrew. This uneducated Scotsman—with no formal divinity training, no university degree, no reputation as a scholar, and with poor ability to speak French—would become the spark that brought revival to Geneva again.

With simple but confident biblical knowledge, Haldane reasoned boldly from the Scriptures. Much like the Savior he proclaimed, Haldane wowed his listeners with the authority of his argumentation (e.g., Matt. 7:29)

---

4. A. L. Drummond, "Robert Haldane at Geneva (1816–17)," *Royal Scottish Church History Society* 9 (1947): 75.

5. For more on Haldane's time in Geneva, see Haldane, *Lives of Robert and James Haldane*, 422ff.; D. MacGregor, "The Haldanes," in *Essays by Ministers of the Free Church of Scotland*, ed. W. Hanna (Edinburgh: Thomas Constable, 1858), 126ff.

6. Drummond, "Robert Haldane at Geneva (1816–17)," 75.

rather than the speculations being made by their divinity professors. And, unlike the divinity professors who clamored to keep their revered and dignified status as Genevan pharisees, Haldane spoke with humble sincerity, further endearing him to the hearts of his disciples. His influence continued to grow.

Haldane centered much of his teaching on Paul's letter to the Romans. He would lecture on the gospel of grace, the role of the law in salvation and in a believer's life, and man's condition outside of grace. Man's natural corruption was an idea completely foreign to the divinity students. One student, J. H. Merle D'Aubigné (who later became a significant evangelical influence in his own right), remembered saying to Haldane, "I now see the doctrine of sin in the Bible," to which Haldane replied, "Yes, my good man, but do you see it in your own heart?" D'Aubigné later recounted how the Holy Spirit used that question to pierce his conscience and lead him to conversion.[7]

Haldane eventually landed back in Scotland, where he would spend the remainder of his life and ministry. Much of his influence was made in his engagement

---

7. Drummond writes of D'Aubigné, "He who had championed his Socinian professors was one day to be a burning and shining light of Continental Evangelicalism." "Robert Haldane at Geneva (1816–17)," 76; cf. L. Maury, *Le Réveil Religieux Dans L'Eglise Reformée à Genève et En France, 1810–1850; Ètude Historique et Dogmatique*, 2 vols. (Paris, 1892).

with various theological controversies and through his voluminous publications. He published his widely influential three-volume commentary on the book of Romans, which was translated into multiple languages and included his treatise on the Sabbath. He engaged unorthodox teachings and liberalizing views wherever he found them, faithfully proclaiming the grace of the gospel until his death in December of 1842.[8] He was buried in Glasgow Cathedral.

Haldane's stalwart defense of an evangelical Calvinism, and his role as mentor to many other men who carried the torch of reformation in Europe, demonstrates his confidence in the principles Paul writes about in 1 Corinthians 1. A man with no formal divinity education, no firm grasp of the language, and no backing from the religious establishment foolishly chose the simple message of Christ crucified. And with that foolish message he not only sparked a revival in Geneva but also showed that the foolishness of God is wiser than man's and the power of God is stronger than man's (1 Cor. 1:25).

---

8. One significant and related example of his engagement with contemporary issues is Haldane's treatise against the opening of the railways on the Sabbath. See his *On the Purposed Desecration of the Sabbath by the Directors of the Edinburgh and Glasgow Railway, with an Appendix Occasioned by a Recent Circular Avowing Their Real Object*, 3rd ed. (Edinburgh: William Whyte & Co., 1842).

Haldane on the Sabbath

Haldane's work on the Sabbath is of particular benefit for believers today. We live in a time when evangelicals have largely dismissed the command to keep the Sabbath holy. Remarkably, we see in Haldane an evangelical leader anticipating and addressing two key difficulties faced by modern skeptics of a Christian Sabbath.

First, Haldane labors to show that the Sabbath principle is not something peculiar to the covenant made with Old Testament Israel. By showing that the Sabbath was mandated before the law of Moses, the moral nature of the Decalogue, and even how the prophets expected Sabbath keeping in the new covenant, Haldane demonstrates the Sabbath principle's abiding validity and permanent obligation for believers.

Second, he presents a compelling examination of the transfer of the Sabbath day from Saturday to Sunday in the new covenant. Many non-Sabbatarians view the transfer of the day as the Achilles' heel of the Sabbatarian position.[9] Haldane, however, demonstrates that the transfer of the day is not only seen in the New Testament but was in fact foreshadowed in the Old Testament. For example, the Old Testament contains

---

9. E.g., see Gaffin's comments in "A Sabbath Rest Still Awaits the People of God," in *Pressing toward the Mark: Essays Commemorating Fifty Years of the Orthodox Presbyterian Church*, ed. Charles G. Dennison and Richard C. Gambel (Philadelphia, Pa.: Committee for the Historian of the Orthodox Presbyterian Church, 1986), 148.

differing motivations for Sabbath observance: Exodus 20 offers creation as the motivation, while Deuteronomy 5 offers redemption, a fact that Haldane believed indicated a forward-looking anticipation to the change of day. Further, all the "eighth day" language of the Old Testament (e.g., circumcision on the eighth day, priestly consecration on the eighth day) found its typological culmination in the resurrection—the eighth day, or first day of a new creation. His arguments remain profitable because they are exegetically nuanced and informed by a firm grasp of biblical theology, no doubt gained through his years of careful study and teaching of the book of Romans.

A Word about This Book

Sanctification of the Sabbath developed from Haldane's exegetical work and was originally added to his Romans commentary as an excurses on Romans 14:5–6. Later, during a controversy surrounding the Scottish railways being run on Sunday, he extracted the essay and published it as a booklet. While Haldane's work on the Lord's Day served as a useful supplement to his exegetical work and an accessible resource in the middle of a dispute, years passed by and it fell into obscurity.

As many of the best research discoveries are made, I stumbled on this gem while digging through an obscure footnote in a relatively unknown document. I was doing research for my dissertation on the Sabbath and happened to read through something Errol Hulse had written years ago on the subject.[10] Hulse mentioned in passing something that Robert Haldane had argued over a hundred and fifty years ago. I decided to follow the footnote, and I'm so glad I did. I believe Haldane to be of great value for us to read today on the topic of the Christian Sabbath. His is the single most helpful treatment I have read on the subject.

In order to make Haldane's essay useful for a broader audience, I decided to extract it once again and present it in the format of this small book. This edition revises and updates the text found in volume 3 of Haldane's 1842 edition of his Romans commentary.[11] I have updated some of the language but have sought to retain as much of Haldane's own voice as possible. I hope that this treatise is as much of a blessing to you as it was to me.

I would be remiss if I didn't express my sincere gratitude to Cody Floate, my friend and former pastoral intern, who helped me greatly with formatting the original Haldane manuscript.

Soli Deo Gloria
Jon English Lee

---

10. Errol Hulse, "Why I Believe in the Sabbath," *Reformation Today*, https://www.reformedontheweb.com/miscellaneous/why-i-believe-in-the-sabbath-hulse.pdf.

11. Robert Haldane, "The Sanctification of the Sabbath," in *Exposition of the Epistle to the Romans* (W. Whyte, 1842), 3:340–402.

Introduction

The general attention which has of late years been drawn to the observance of the Sabbath cannot fail to be the subject of congratulation with every Christian. The importance of the institution is fully perceived only by those who tremble at the Word of God; yet every reflecting mind is compelled to acknowledge that whether as regards mental or physical exertion, some such interval of rest is necessary for the well-being of society. But no argument, however cogent, unless immediately derived from the Scriptures of truth is sufficient to establish the obligation to sanctify the seventh day which must always be rested on the authority of God. It is, therefore, of great moment that the divine character of the sabbatical institution should be distinctly understood, and the more so because many have been led to imagine that it is a mere Jewish ordinance unrecognized in the New Testament and even set aside or in a measure superseded by our Lord and His apostles as in chapter 14:5–6 of the epistle to the Romans. This is a most pernicious error—an error exhibiting great ignorance of spiritual things and one highly calculated to retard the progress of the Christian in the divine life. The apostles, when speaking of days which might or might not be observed without sin, obviously alluded to holy days peculiar to the Jewish economy, and with it about to vanish away; but the Sabbath was set apart from the beginning of the world and was therefore intended to be held equally holy under the patriarchal, the Jewish, and the Christian dispensations.

In proving the duty of Christians to hallow the Lord's Day, it is necessary to show that there is nothing in this duty peculiar to the law of Moses, but that it rests on the permanent obligation of the original institution, afterward embodied in the Decalogue, and also recognized by our Lord and His apostles. It is necessary, also, to prove that the change of the day from the last to the first day of the week has not made void the import of the primary institution or of the fourth commandment, whose binding and permanent authority is by no means affected by that change. If it could be ascertained that the Sabbath is not appointed to be observed on the first day of the week, the consequence would be not that we should be freed from its obligation, but that we ought to sanctify it on the original day. This would be incumbent on all the posterity of Adam to the end of the world.

We are taught that it is the reasonable service of every intelligent creature to hold all that he possesses at the disposal of "Him in whom we live, and move, and have our being." In paradise a grant was made to man of the fruits of the earth with one reservation; after the flood this grant was renewed and extended, and without such a grant it would have been an act of robbery for man to seize upon any one of the productions of his Maker. The same is true in regard to our time. Every minute belongs to God, and it is for the Almighty to determine in what manner we are to number and employ our days. On this subject He has not left mankind in ignorance but has instituted the ordinance of weekly rest and commanded it to be observed according to His appointment.

– 1 –

The Sabbath Anterior to the Mosaic Dispensation

The Sabbath neither originated nor ceased with the law of Moses. It was instituted immediately after the creation before man had sinned, and for a reason that has no dependence on that economy. "And on the seventh day God ended His work which He had done, and He rested on the seventh day from all His work which He had done. Then God blessed the seventh day and sanctified it, because in it He rested from all His work which God had created and made" (Gen. 2:2–3). Here a reason is given for the sanctification of the seventh day unconnected with anything local or temporary; and the blessing pronounced on it, as well as its sanctification, implies that it is blessed and sanctified for man. All the days of creation were good. None of them was cursed or unholy—the seventh day, therefore, was not blessed and sanctified on account of possessing any natural superiority or preeminence. It was sanctified by a command to Adam, and through him to all his posterity to keep it holy as a day set apart and blessed by the Creator on which He rested from His work; and this is the reason given in the fourth commandment, more than two thousand years afterward, for sanctifying this day. If, then, on a certain account, one day of the week is declared to be blessed and sanctified, it must be distinguished from the other days and a peculiar blessing must rest upon it. Are, then, the Jews alone concerned in this? What exclusive connection has such a Sabbath with Jewish institutions of a mere temporary nature? Are not all men in all ages equally interested in it? If, even in a state of innocence, the Sabbath was a blessing to man, how much more is it necessary for him in a state of sin, degradation, and toil?

Two great laws were delivered to man at the beginning, in both of which God asserted His sovereignty. The first was the appointment of the Sabbath, or a seventh day's rest. The second was the law of marriage. These two ordinances were instituted as a basis of that relation which was to subsist between God and man and of every relative connection among men. There were ordinances coeval in their appointment with the existence of the human race upon the earth, and must subsist while man has a being upon it.

Notwithstanding the proof from the words of the institution, Genesis 2:2, that the Sabbath was to be universally observed, it has been urged by those who impugn its authority that no mention is made of it during the patriarchal ages, and therefore that it cannot then have been in force. But, considering the nature and

Anterior to the Mosaic Dispensation

brevity of the Scripture history, even were it true that no intimation is given respecting the Sabbath in that period, this would furnish no valid argument against its existence. In several books of the Old Testament, even in those where the omission was hardly to have been anticipated, the Sabbath is not mentioned, although in the periods in which they were written it continued to be regularly observed. Numerous allusions, however, are from the beginning and all along to be found to the Sabbath. Besides many others, the division of time into weeks of seven days may be noticed, and the frequent introduction of the number seven, as even in the short account of the flood [Gen. 7:2, 3, 4, 10; 8:10, 12], relating both to the causal occurrences and to the worship of God. The number seven is expressed in Hebrew by a word signifying fullness, perfection, or completion; and to this number it may be further observed, a sacred character has been attached from the earliest ages, among all nations, whether idolaters or worshipers of the true God. But even if no mention had been made of the observance of the Sabbath, and no allusion to it had been found during the patriarchal ages or at any other period, its binding obligation would remain unimpaired since the institution itself, and the ground on which it rests, are so fully declared at the commencement of the Scriptures as to render any recurrence to the subject in the way of authority unnecessary.

In the account of the gathering of the manna, Exodus 16:4, before the law was delivered from Sinai, we have satisfactory evidence of the obligation to observe the Sabbath day: "Then the LORD said to Moses, 'Behold, I will rain bread from heaven for you. And the people shall go out and gather a certain quota every day, that I may test them, whether they will walk in My law or not. And it shall be on the sixth day that they shall prepare what they bring in, and it shall be twice as much as they gather daily.'" Here is direct reference to a "law" previously existing, by which God was to prove the obedience of the Israelites, and here also is a clear intimation that the law referred to required the separation of the seventh from the other days of the week. On the Sabbath they were to rest; on the Sabbath they were not to gather the manna, and, in the providence of God, it was declared that this should not be necessary, for God would give them as much on the sixth day as would also suffice for the seventh. Accordingly, it is said (vv. 22–26),

> And so it was, on the sixth day, that they gathered twice as much bread, two omers for each one. And all the rulers of the congregation came and told Moses. Then he said to them, "This is what the LORD has said: 'Tomorrow is a Sabbath rest, a holy Sabbath to the LORD. Bake what you will bake today, and boil what you will boil; and lay up for yourselves all that remains, to be kept until morning.'" So they laid it up till morning, as Moses commanded; and it did not stink, nor were

there any worms in it. Then Moses said, "Eat that today, for today is a Sabbath to the LORD; today you will not find it in the field. Six days you shall gather it, but on the seventh day, the Sabbath, there will be none."

When, notwithstanding this injunction, some of the people went out on the seventh day to gather the manna, "The LORD," it is added (vv. 28–30), "said to Moses, 'How long do you refuse to keep My commandments and My laws? See! For the LORD has given you the Sabbath; therefore He gives you on the sixth day bread for two days. Let every man remain in his place; let no man go out of his place on the seventh day.' So the people rested on the seventh day." Here is express mention of the seventh day, and of the Sabbath, and reference to God's laws and commandments, previously given, respecting it. The Sabbath, it is observed, too, is spoken of in the past time (the Lord has given) and the manna in the present (He gives), while the Sabbath, formerly given, is declared to be the reason why there was twice as much manna on the sixth day. "The LORD has given you the Sabbath; therefore He gives you on the sixth day bread for two days." In all this we have clear proof of the previous existence of a "law"—namely, "the rest of the holy Sabbath." This law was imposed on Adam when he stood as the representative of the whole human race and is consequently binding on all his posterity. We may here observe that three miracles in honor of the Sabbath, and to secure it against desecration, were wrought every week before the promulgation of the law. Double the quantity of manna fell every sixth day. None fell on the Sabbath. The manna preserved for that day did not corrupt. We have thus seen that the duty of the sanctification of the Sabbath was enjoined before the existence of the Mosaic dispensation; it shall now be proved that it remains in force since that dispensation has passed away.

–2–

The Sabbath Binding Alike under the Jewish and Christian Dispensations

The duty of the observance of the Sabbath, resting on the original institution, forms a part of the Ten Commandments, and on this account also is of permanent and universal obligation. It is most erroneous to suppose that because these commandments were delivered to the Israelites that for them they were exclusively intended. To the Jews were committed the oracles of God, and they were appointed His witnesses to all nations (Isa. 43:10, 12). It is therefore necessary to distinguish between the general laws delivered to Israel as a testimony for all mankind and those national laws—the statutes and the judgments—which were peculiar to that people. All the other nations had fallen into idolatry because "they did not like to retain God in their knowledge." From these the Israelites were separated in order that by them the worship of the true Jehovah might be maintained and, above all, that from among them the Messiah should spring. For the purpose of continuing this separation, as well as of rendering it subservient to the future dispensation, the law in its various parts—moral, ceremonial, and judicial—was delivered to Israel. The moral law, contained in the Ten Commandments, was, from its nature, of universal and permanent obligation, while the laws that were political, ritual, or ceremonial had previously no existence and were to be abrogated when their destined end was accomplished. But the Decalogue, on which these other laws were grounded, the sum of which is the love of God and of our neighbor, containing the eternal rule of right and wrong, had been in force from the beginning and must forever continue immutable. It was accordingly distinguished from the other laws in a very remarkable manner, both in its promulgation and in its preservation.

The Manner of the Promulgation of the Decalogue

The Ten Commandments alone were promulgated by the voice of God amid the most manifest tokens of the divine presence and majesty. They were delivered to a whole nation, who trembled when they heard them and solemnly promised obedience. When they were proclaimed, Moses and Aaron only were present on the mount, which the people and the priests were forbidden even to touch. And as these commandments had been pronounced by the voice of God, in the hearing of all the people, they were also written by the finger of God on two tables of stone, while the other laws were delivered to Moses only and written by him in a book. "These words the LORD spoke to all your assembly, in the mountain from the midst of the fire, the cloud, and the thick darkness, with a loud voice; and He added no more. And He wrote them on two tablets of stone and gave them to me" (Deut. 5:22). Such were the striking peculiarities of the promulgation of the Ten Commandments.

The two tables of the law were given to Moses on the mount, but before he returned to the people they had violated and trampled on its great commandment. Moses, in consequence, cast the tables out of his hand and broke them, thus significantly indicating that the law given to man had been broken and that, if committed to his keeping, by him it could not be fulfilled. With man this was impossible, but with God all things are possible. It was His eternal purpose, purposed in Christ Jesus, that His law should notwithstanding be fulfilled and that by His own power this fulfillment should be accomplished. Moses was therefore commanded to prepare two new tables, on which God again wrote "the words that were on the first tablets" (Ex. 34:1), which He delivered once more into the hand of Moses; but in doing so not even Aaron, and no man but Moses, representing on that occasion the one Mediator between God and man, was allowed to go up or to be seen throughout all the mount. "And the LORD passed before him and proclaimed, "The LORD, the LORD God, merciful and gracious, long-suffering, and abounding in goodness and truth, keeping mercy for thousands, forgiving iniquity and transgression and sin, by no means clearing the guilty" (Ex. 34:6–7). It was thus declared that through the goodness and mercy of God, sin, the transgression of the law, should be pardoned, but that this should be effected in consistency with His holiness and justice, that the sinner should be forgiven, but sin should not go unpunished.

–4–

The Manner of the Preservation of the Decalogue and the Lessons Thereby Taught

In the manner of their preservation, the Ten Commandments were as much distinguished from all the other laws given to Israel as they had been in the mode of their promulgation. A tabernacle was prepared for their reception, by the special direction of God, and within it an ark placed, in which the two tables of the law were to be deposited. The ark, formed of the most durable wood, was overlaid with gold, within and without. It was called the ark of the covenant, and over it was placed the mercy seat, that eminent type of the Mediator of the new covenant. On this mercy seat the divine glory was to descend, and thence as from a throne Jehovah was to hold communication with His people. When the tabernacle was "set up," the ark, covered with a veil, was placed in it and Aaron and his sons were consecrated. When this was done, Moses "took the Testimony and put it into the ark, inserted the poles through the rings of the ark, and put the mercy seat on top of the ark. And he brought the ark into the tabernacle, hung up the veil of the covering, and partitioned off the ark of the Testimony, as the LORD had commanded Moses" (Ex. 40:20–21).

Similar solemnities were observed when the ark was transferred from the tabernacle to the temple.

> Then the priests brought in the ark of the covenant of the LORD to its place, into the inner sanctuary of the temple, to the Most Holy Place, under the wings of the cherubim. For the cherubim spread their two wings over the place of the ark, and the cherubim overshadowed the ark and its poles. The poles extended so that the ends of the poles could be seen from the holy place, in front of the inner sanctuary; but they could not be seen from outside. And they are there to this day. Nothing was in the ark except the two tablets of stone which Moses put there at Horeb, when the LORD made a covenant with the children of Israel, when they came out of the land of Egypt. (1 Kings 8:6–9)

Into the holy of holies, in which were the ark and the mercy seat, the high priest alone entered, and that only once every year, after offering a solemn sacrifice of atonement for himself and all the people, and the punishment of death was denounced against him if he entered at any other time; and at no time was any other man allowed to enter. Even in the tabernacle there was to be no man when he made the atonement (Lev. 16:17). When the tabernacle was to be removed, Aaron and his sons were to take down the covering veil, cover the ark of the testimony with it, and to put two more coverings over it. "Then the sons of Kohath shall come to carry them; but they shall not touch any holy thing, lest they die" (Num. 4:15). It was death to touch the ark. Uzzah was smitten with death for putting his hand to it (2 Sam. 6:7). It was death to look into it. "Then He struck the men of Beth Shemesh, because they had looked into the ark of the LORD. He struck fifty thousand and seventy men of the people" (1 Sam. 6:19). Both these examples contain most salutary instruction to those who have fled to Christ for refuge and to all who are yet in their sins. To this hour it is death to look, in a spirit of self-righteousness, on that law which the ark contained. It is death to look on it, except through Him who is the end of the law for righteousness to everyone that believeth.

The importance attached to the tabernacle and the ark containing the Ten Commandments, and these alone, demands particular attention. While the history of the creation of the universe—of the earth, the sun, the moon, and the stars—is related by the sacred historian in one short chapter, the account of the construction of the tabernacle and the ark is detailed in thirteen. In his account of the creation of the universe, Moses is brief and general; in that of the construction of the tabernacle and the ark he is copious and records the smallest peculiarities. The world was created in order that God should be glorified by the church and that by it His manifold wisdom might be made known unto the principalities and powers in heavenly places according to the eternal purpose which He purposed in Christ Jesus our Lord (Eph. 3:10). In the tabernacle and the ark His law was to be deposited, till by the coming of His Son it should be fulfilled for the redemption of His people from its curse; and, accordingly, the construction of the tabernacle and the ark is spoken of more amply and more particularly than the formation of all the elements and all the universe.

The remarkable prominence thus given to the construction of the tabernacle, and the extraordinary precautions regarding the ark as subservient to the conservation of the holy law, prove its importance in the sight of God—of that everlasting law by which He governs the world, which is holy, just, good, and which in its substance must be eternally binding on all intelligent creatures, both men and angels. This law had been broken by man. But, though broken and dishonored, its authority was in due time to be vindicated, not merely by the infliction of its awful penalty but also by the fulfillment of its holy precepts, and that, too, upon earth, which had been the scene of its violation. Had not this been the purpose of God, we may be assured that the law would never again have been promulgated to man. Nothing would have remained but a fearful looking for of judgment and of fiery indignation to consume its transgressors. But God in the midst of wrath remembered mercy. Glory to God in the highest was at length, through the fulfilling of this law, to be proclaimed, and on earth peace and good will toward men.

In the renewal of the tables of the law, accompanied with the proclamation of the mercy of God and their being placed in the ark covered with the mercy seat, intimation was given of that future fulfillment of the law and the removal of its curse. In other words, it was intimated that a righteousness adequate to all its demands, which could not be performed by man, should be provided by God. And this solemn transaction, and the purposed fulfillment of its import, were, in the fortieth psalm, prophetically declared of Him who alone could bring in this righteousness, where He Himself announces His coming to do His Father's will.

> Behold, I come;
> In the scroll of the book it is written of me.
> I delight to do Your will, O my God,
> And Your law is within my heart.
>
> I have proclaimed the good news of righteousness
> In the great assembly;
> Indeed, I do not restrain my lips,
> O LORD, You Yourself know.
> I have not hidden Your righteousness within my
> heart. (vv. 7–10)

Here we are made acquainted with the reason why the holy law was promulgated by the voice of Jehovah Himself with the sound of a trumpet, amid thunderings and lightnings from the mountain that burned with fire, and proclaimed in this awful manner as a testimony to all nations and every age of the world: why, after being broken, the tables of the law were renewed and deposited in the tabernacle and the ark; why such importance was attached to them for its preservation; and why such solemn prohibitions respecting them were added, backed by the sanction of instant death. This "fiery law," thus covered from the eye of man, was like the book, sealed with seven seals, which no man in heaven nor on earth was found worthy to open, neither to look therein. The lion of the tribe of Judah, the Lamb in the midst of the throne, who alone could look upon that book, alone could fulfill that holy law. He only could magnify and make it honorable. He only could "bring in everlasting righteousness"—a righteousness performed in time but to endure throughout eternity—consisting at once in suffering the penalty which man by transgression had incurred, and in the fulfillment of the precept, which he had failed to obey. His obedience in this double respect reaches infinitely beyond the power of all created beings, and furnishes of itself incontestable proof, were none besides to be found in the book of God, that Jesus Christ was "God manifest in the flesh," "Emmanuel, God with us," "Jehovah our righteousness."

That there was no other way in which God's law could be fulfilled, after it had been broken, is certain, since God does nothing in vain. If in any other way this could have been accomplished, the highest of all

The Preservation of the Decalogue

means—as the incarnation of His Son must appear in the eye of every one who believes that He is "over all, God blessed forever"—would not have been employed. The language of our Lord Himself was, "O My Father, if it is possible, let this cup pass from Me." It did not pass from Him, and this demonstrates that by no other possible means could the law have been fulfilled and the work of man's salvation accomplished. The truth and the faithfulness of God required that the honor of His violated law should be vindicated by the infliction of its penalty, according to His express declaration to the first man if it should be transgressed. Sin, therefore, must have been punished either in the person of the sinner or of a Surety in his place, and as it was impossible that any mere creature, even of the highest possible order, could be such a surety, either the incarnation of the Son of God or the punishment of the transgressor was inevitable. The fulfillment of the law, however, by His Son did not leave it to be afterward abrogated or trampled on by those who should receive the benefit of His vicarious obedience, while its nature forbade its being changed or relaxed in the smallest degree, which would render it neither holy nor just and consequently unworthy of God. There are many, notwithstanding, who maintain that, under the new covenant, the requirements of this holy law are modified or lowered, so as to be adapted to that degree of obedience which can be yielded by fallen man. This most destructive error, degrading to the character of God, utterly at variance with His holiness and justice, supposing the introduction of one evil to remedy another, gives an entirely false view of the plan of redemption. It is subversive of the law; for not only, if it failed to require perfect holiness, would it cease to be a holy law but it would cease to be in any sense a law. Could that be called a law which did not demand obedience to its own requirements, and which would not be violated when they were disobeyed? Did ever such a law exist? Does not every law, whether divine or human, even respecting things of the least value, require implicit and perfect obedience? Can anyone show what are the requirements of that mitigated law of which some so ignorantly speak, or where it is to be found?

In the plan of salvation, it is true, provision is made for God's acceptance of the services of His children, although as coming from them they are imperfect, in other words, alloyed with sin, and so falling short of the divine requirements. But on what ground are they accepted? Is it on their own account? If so, it would indeed be at the expense of the perfection of the law. But it is far otherwise. As the high priest of Israel made atonement for the uncleanness of the people, so the services of believers are presented to God by their Great High Priest, through whose atonement and intercession the sin that cleaves to them is entirely removed. "'In those days and in that time,' says the LORD, 'The iniquity of Israel shall be sought, but there shall be none; and the

The Preservation of the Decalogue

sins of Judah, but they shall not be found; for I will pardon those whom I preserve.'" Washed in that fountain opened for sin and for uncleanness, they are presented faultless by Him who is their Surety—in other words, as entirely conformed to the perfect standard of God's holy law. The duty of believers is to be perfect, even as their Father which is in heaven is perfect; but as in all things and in every moment they come short, their imperfections are not set aside by lowering the requirements of the law of God or by expunging any part of it, but are altogether removed in a way that to the utmost honors that law, satisfying its highest demands by Him with whom they are one. God, then, is "a just God and a Savior"; but this He could not be if, in the plan of salvation, He either abrogated or lowered His law, dispensed with the perfect obedience to it of those who are saved, pardoned their sins without an atonement, or accepted their persons or services in any other way than that in which the law is "fulfilled" in them (Rom. 8:4). Well might the apostle say, "Do we then make void the law through faith? Certainly not! On the contrary, we establish the law" (Rom. 3:31).

Proof of the Permanence of the Fourth Commandment Derived from the Foregoing Statements

It having been the purpose of God that the dishonor done to His law in its violation should be repaired in a way in which it is exhibited as more glorious and more highly valued by Him than ever it had been before, ought not means to have been used forcibly to impress this on the minds of men, till that reparation should take place? The precautions, therefore, employed for the preservation of the two tables of the law—after the first had been broken, which in any other view would, from their strictness and minuteness, be altogether unaccountable—were admirably adapted to the end for which they were appointed. Here, then, we have a demonstration of the permanent obligation of the fourth commandment of the Decalogue, since it constitutes a part of that law which was so signally distinguished in its promulgation and so carefully deposited for its preservation—of that law which the Redeemer fulfilled for the justification of His people; and that law by which they are justified, they must be bound in all its parts to obey. How, then, shall it ever be supposed that the Ten Commandments belonged only to Israel, and are not of everlasting and universal obligation? Or on what ground can it be affirmed that the fourth commandment is to be separated from the rest, so that one is blotted out of their number and that they are now reduced to nine?

Here let us for a moment pause and consider how God, in the redemption of His people and the forgiveness of their sins through the blood of Christ, has abounded toward them in all wisdom and prudence. The manner in which these blessings are provided is at once most humbling and most consolatory. Their communion with their heavenly Father is secured, but the way in which it is obtained lays them low in the dust. All the glory redounds to God, while the richest benefits are conferred on man. Here, too, the conclusion to which the apostle conducts his argument in the epistle to the Hebrews is strikingly applicable. There he had established the superiority of the new covenant over that first covenant which made nothing perfect and had vanished away, during which "the way into the Holiest of All was not yet made manifest" (Heb. 9:8); and he sums up the whole in the following consolatory exhortation: "Therefore, brethren, having boldness to enter the Holiest by the blood of Jesus, by a new and living way which He consecrated for us, through the veil, that is, His flesh, and having a High Priest over the house of God, let us draw near with a true heart in full assurance of faith" (Heb. 10:19–22).

On the whole, it is evident that the Ten Commandments in no respect exclusively belonged, like the other laws, to the nation of Israel. These laws, written in a book (Deut. 31:9, 24, 26), were delivered to them for their keeping and placed at the side of the ark. But after the first tables on which the Ten Commandments had been inscribed were broken, the renewed tables, guarded by the most awful sanctions, were put within the ark and covered even from their sight. They were deposited beneath the mercy seat, in the tabernacle, the "habitation" of the Lord, and afterward in the temple and brought "in the ark of the covenant of the LORD to its place, into the inner sanctuary of the temple, to the Most Holy Place" (2 Chron. 5:7). Nor was this holy sanctuary laid open, and exposed to view, until He who had fulfilled every jot and tittle of the law said it is finished. The veil of the temple was then rent in twain from the top to the bottom. The mystery of the ark, and the Ten Commandments deposited in it, was unfolded and the way into the holiest of all made manifest. These commandments are moral in their nature, requiring what is applicable to men in every age, and in the heart of this universal and eternal law the fourth commandment is embodied. We are thus taught that the Sabbath is not a mere ceremonial institution, that it is on the contrary a command of moral obligation, regulating by divine authority the disposal of our time, teaching us how much we may devote to the world and how much we are to reserve for God. Those who imagine that such a commandment is of a transient or ceremonial character have very ill considered the words in which it is couched, the duty which it is designed to inculcate, or the sanction by which it is enforced.

–6–

Internal Evidence Shows That the Fourth Commandment Is of Universal Obligation

The fourth commandment contains in itself sufficient proof that it did not exclusively belong to the Mosaic dispensation but that the duty it enjoins was at all times binding on man from the period of his creation. This is evident from the reason by which the duty of its observance is enforced. It contains not a word peculiar to the nation of Israel but founds on the fact common to all mankind, that God rested on the seventh day from the work of creation and blessed and sanctified it, repeating the very words of the original institution and thus recognizing and enforcing its universal and permanent authority. From this it is manifest that the duty to sanctify the Sabbath is not confined to any particular age or nation but that, while God has given to man what are called by the prophet Ezekiel "the six working days" (46:1), He has reserved the seventh for His own immediate service. It may likewise be remarked that Israel was called on in the fourth commandment to remember the Sabbath day. This supposes antecedent knowledge, and implies that it was no new institution delivered for them, but one of a former period of which they needed to be put in remembrance.

In the same way Nehemiah 9:13–14 speaks of the Sabbath as not newly appointed when promulgated to the Jews: "You came down also on Mount Sinai, and spoke with them from heaven, and gave them just ordinances and true laws, good statutes and commandments. You made known to them Your holy Sabbath, and commanded them precepts, statutes and laws, by the hand of Moses Your servant." Here we observe the difference of expression with regard to the Sabbath from that used respecting the judgments and precepts and statutes. These He gave and commanded, but His holy Sabbath He made known to them. This shows that the Sabbath, so remarkably distinguished as God's holy Sabbath, had been previously promulgated and that God then restored the full knowledge of it.

The fourth commandment is closely connected with the other commandments; but so far from having any Jewish origin, it is the first and only commandment announced in the opening of the sacred record and was imposed on our first parents in their state of uprightness and innocence. It thus stands in a peculiar manner at the head of all the commandments and involves in its breach the abandonment equally of the first and second tables of the Decalogue. It is placed at the end of the first table, as the tenth is at the end of the second, as the

Internal Evidence of Universal Obligation 31

safeguard of all the rest. It stands between the two tables of our duty to God and our duty to man as the great foundation and cornerstone binding both together—its observance supporting and conducing to our obedience to the whole. It is placed as the guardian of the first and second commandments, in which the Lord is asserted to be our God, and of the third, which prohibits the profanation of His holy name. This connection with the first and second commandments is recognized: "You shall not make idols for yourselves; neither a carved image nor a sacred pillar shall you rear up for yourselves; nor shall you set up an engraved stone in your land, to bow down to it; for I am the LORD your God" (Lev. 26:1). In like manner it is said, "Do not walk in the statutes of your fathers, nor observe their judgments, nor defile yourselves with their idols. I am the LORD your God: Walk in My statutes, keep My judgments, and do them; hallow My Sabbaths" (Ezek. 20:18–20). The fourth commandment is likewise introduced to enforce the other commandments, both of the first and second table. In the nineteenth chapter of Leviticus, which opens with this general exhortation to holiness, "Speak to all the congregation of the children of Israel, and say to them: 'You shall be holy, for I the LORD your God am holy,'" obedience to the fifth commandment is immediately after enjoined and enforced by the fourth: "Every one of you shall revere his mother and his father, and keep My Sabbaths." Other commandments, both of the first and second tables, are in the same chapter likewise specified. "You shall not steal, nor deal falsely, nor lie to one another. And you shall not swear by My name falsely, nor shall you profane the name of your God" (vv. 11–12). And after referring to various laws of the second table, and giving the summary of the whole of it, "You shall love your neighbor as yourself" (v. 18), the fourth commandment, as connected with them all, is again brought into view: "You shall keep My Sabbaths and reverence My sanctuary: I am the LORD" (v. 30). In this chapter, as Archdeacon Stopford, in his Scripture account of the Sabbath, observes, "We find the Sabbath in connection with the 1st, 2nd, and 3rd commandments of the first table, and with the 5th, 6th, 7th, 8th, and 9th of the second. The 10th is not mentioned, being itself a guard or fence round the other commandments of the second table."

Objections to the Permanent Obligation of the Sabbath Considered

In contending against the obligation of the Sabbath as a duty universally binding, it has been urged that the preface to the Ten Commandments shows that they were incumbent only on the Jews. "I am the LORD your God, who brought you out of the land of Egypt, out of the house of bondage." This is no proof that these commandments were intended exclusively for the Israelites, but it shows a peculiar reason why they, above all men, should observe them, since God had given them deliverance from the slavery of Egypt. In addition, then, to the commemoration of the rest from the work of creation, there was to the Israelites this other reason, that they had obtained rest from slavery. And as their slavery in Egypt and deliverance from bondage were typical of the slavery of sin and deliverance by Christ, so the Sabbath to the Israelites, besides being binding on them according to the original and universal institution, was a type of the rest that was to come.

It has likewise been alleged in opposition to the universally binding obligation of the Sabbath that its sanctions prove that it was a Jewish institution. The Israelites were commanded to keep it by the sanction of death (Ex. 31:14; Num. 15:35). This has no necessary connection with the Sabbath. The Sabbath was incorporated with the Mosaic law, and in that situation it partook of the nature of that dispensation. The law was a yoke added because of transgressions. The sanction, then, of the Sabbath, when incorporated with the law, was agreeable to the nature of the law, and not a part of its original institution. The sanction of death which, in the Mosaic law, was likewise added to some of the other commandments, on account of which no one pleads that they have become void, was not originally annexed to the breach of the Sabbath, nor any other peculiarity that related to the Israelites, to whom, besides its institution in the general law, it was also "a sign" of their special relation to God (Ex. 31:13–17; Ezek. 20:12–20); and therefore this sanction belonging to their peculiar laws is not to be identified with the originally instituted Sabbath. Marriage was an ordinance of God from the beginning, coeval with that of the sanctification of the seventh day; but marriage had some peculiarities among the Jews, such as the marrying of the brother's wife, which is done away. Shall we say, because these peculiarities are done away, that the ordinance of marriage which was established in the garden of Eden is done away with the law of Moses? Objections to the permanent obligation of the Sabbath have been drawn from certain expressions in the New Testament, as for example from what is said in Colossians 2:16 and the verses that follow. But in that place the apostle is cautioning those whom he addresses against returning to the observance of Jewish ordinances, declaring that they were "a shadow of things to come." He guards them against these as "basic principles of the world" and directs them to Christ, in whom believers are "complete" without the addition of those ordinances which only prefigured Him. After declaring that Christ had blotted out "the handwriting of requirements that was against us, which was contrary to us. And He has taken it out of the way, having nailed it to the cross," he adds in the verse from which the objection is taken, "Let no one judge you in food or in drink, or regarding a festival or a new moon or sabbaths, which are a shadow of things to come." Here he connects the days of which he speaks with abstinence from certain meats, just as he does in Romans 14:5–6, all the distinctions respecting which were done away. The word, too, rendered *Sabbaths*, is often applied to the days of the week. Besides the weekly Sabbath, it means also the Jewish Sabbaths which accompanied the feasts. The word rendered *holy day* signifies a feast day—one of the Jewish festivals. This word is in the singular, although *Sabbaths* is plural, and the meaning is a feast day, with its accompanying Sabbaths.

In the epistle to the Galatians (4:10), Paul employs language respecting the observance of particular days, similar to that in Romans 14, and Colossians 2—"You observe days and months and seasons and years"—and calls them the weak and beggarly elements, whereunto they desired again to be in bondage. But that among these "days" he did not include the weekly Sabbath, which never could be so characterized, we have the most unquestionable proof; for, in another epistle, 1 Corinthians 16:2, he commands that the first day of the week should be particularly distinguished and observed and intimates that he had enjoined the same on the churches of the Galatians, whom, as we see, he had reprehended on account of their observance of particular days.

Those passages in the New Testament, then, which speak of setting aside the observance of certain days, or of all days being alike, refer to the Sabbaths that were observed by the Jews, distinct from the weekly Sabbath. These were a shadow, and when that which they prefigured was accomplished, they were done away. But the observance of the Sabbath itself is like all the other commandments, of moral and permanent obligation.

It has been objected to the permanent obligation of the fourth commandment that the Lord Jesus Christ has relaxed or modified its requirements, but for this there is no foundation. He came, as He Himself declares, not to destroy but fulfill the law and the prophets. All the types and shadows and ritual observances, as well as the testimony of the prophets, found in Him their accomplishment. But the grand object of His coming into the world, to which these were subservient, was to magnify and make honorable the law of everlasting obligation, and thus He was to be the end of the law for righteousness to everyone that believeth. Accordingly, He fulfilled that law, summed up in the Ten Commandments, promulgated by the voice of God and preserved in a manner so peculiar. Of that law, the sanctifying of one day in seven to the service of God is a part, and as we have seen not only a constituent but a very prominent part, and like all its other parts was forever to remain in force.

The Lord Jesus honored the Sabbath on all occasions by attending the institutions of public worship, and on that day working many of His most distinguished miracles, while He vindicated it from unauthorized traditions contrary to its real design. When charged with breaking the Sabbath, He justified His conduct not by speaking of it as a temporary observance or one that was to be abolished or modified but in a way in which its permanency was assumed and to show that its obligation was to remain unimpaired. His explanations respecting it were entirely consistent with the requirements of the fourth commandment. If, in expounding these and setting aside the false glosses annexed to them, He had intended to teach that the Sabbath was not to be observed with such strictness in His kingdom as the law demanded, He would not have vindicated His conduct by proving that He was acting in conformity to its precepts from the beginning. When the Pharisees charged Him with doing what was not lawful on the Sabbath day, instead of showing any disposition to set aside or relax its obligations, He referred them to their own practice of loosing their ox from the stall and leading it away to watering and asked, whether if it had fallen into a pit, they would not straightway pull it out on the Sabbath day. He inquired if they did not know what David did when he was hungry, and again, if they had not read in the law that on the Sabbath days the priests in the temple profaned the Sabbath and were blameless. By justifying His own conduct in this manner, and referring to what had all along been practiced under the law, He showed that it was not His purpose to set aside the obligation of the Sabbath, or in any degree to change it, but to refer them to its true import, according to which those very acts of necessity and mercy were allowed, on account of which the Jews upbraided Him and His disciples. In doing, then, what had formerly been practiced without any infraction of the law, He was not interfering with its ancient and acknowledged obligation.

That the Lord did not purpose to abolish the Sabbath day is evident from His referring to the continuance of the Sabbath, when all obligation to observe it as a Jewish institution had ceased. In foretelling the destruction of Jerusalem, and referring to the flight not of Jews but of His disciples, at a time when everything peculiar to the Jewish dispensation would be abrogated, He directs them to pray that it might not be in the winter, neither on the Sabbath day (Matt. 24:20), which, from the nature of the season and their sense of the obligation of the fourth commandment, would impede their flight. Henry, in his note on this passage, observes,

> This intimates Christ's design, that a weekly Sabbath should be observed in his church, after the preaching of the gospel to all the world. We read not of any of the ordinances of the Jewish church, which were purely ceremonial, that Christ ever expressed any care about, because they were all to vanish; but for the Sabbath he often showed a concern. It intimates, likewise, that the Sabbath is ordinarily to be observed as a day of rest from travel and worldly labor; but that, according to his own explication of the fourth commandment, works of necessity were lawful on the Sabbath day, as that of fleeing from an enemy to save our lives. But it intimates, likewise, that it is very uneasy and uncomfortable to a good man to be taken off by any work of necessity from the solemn service and worship of God on the Sabbath day. We should pray that we may have quiet and undisturbed Sabbaths, and may have no other work than Sabbath work to do on the Sabbath days, that we may attend upon the Lord without distraction. To flee in the winter is uncomfortable to the body; but to flee on the Sabbath day is so to the soul, and the more so when it remembers former Sabbaths; as Ps. 42:4.

While nothing in the discourses or conduct of our Lord tends to set aside or relax the duty of obedience to the fourth commandment, He has confirmed its permanent obligation by frequently appealing to the authority of the Decalogue, by which He established every part of it. When asked what was the first of all the commandments (Mark 12:28), He gave the substance of the first table as Moses had given it (Deut. 6:5) and that of the second in the words which Moses had used when summing up various duties arising out of it (Lev. 19:18). On another occasion, when He put the question to a certain lawyer, "What is written in the law? What is your reading of it?" (Luke 10:26), the reply was the same as Jesus Himself had given in the case just referred to and was approved of by Him: "So he answered and said, '"You shall love the LORD your God with all your heart, with all your soul, with all your strength, and with all your mind," and "your neighbor as yourself."' And He said to him, 'You have answered rightly; do this and you will live.'" From this it follows that, by adopting the same summaries of the law with Moses whom He quoted, and with the other Jews, our Lord referred to the same commandments, even the moral law contained in the Ten Commandments. And lest anyone might suppose that He spoke only of the Mosaic dispensation, He added to the summary He had just given, "On these two commandments hang all the Law and the Prophets" (Matt. 22:40); that is, on these two commandments or summaries of the two tables depend not only the Mosaic dispensation but also the prophets, or that dispensation which was to come, which is the subject of the prophecies. When asked by the rich young man what he should do to inherit eternal life, Jesus answered, "If you want to enter into life, keep the commandments." He thus showed that it was not to anything peculiar to the law of Moses but to the commandments He referred, by distinguishing them by that name and specifying those of the second table, which, on the occasion above quoted, He had said was like unto the first.

As the Lord Himself sanctioned the permanent obligation of the law of the Decalogue, His apostles likewise maintained its authority. The apostle James, in quoting two of the commandments, refers to the whole law. Paul quotes the fifth, calling it the first commandment with promise (Eph. 6:2). In thus referring to one of these commandments as binding on Christians, and as known by them to be so, and thereby enforcing what he enjoins, he establishes the authority of the whole of them. It is also to be remarked that, by thus calling the attention of the Gentile Christians at Ephesus to the promised blessing, he shows that this promise was not designed to apply exclusively to the land of Canaan or the children of Israel. In the same way, in the epistle to the Romans (13:9), he enjoins the duty of love to our neighbor by quoting those commandments of the second table which relate to that duty. And in the epistle to the Galatians (5:14), he gives the same summary of the second table as Moses and our Lord had given: "You shall love your neighbor as yourself." It is to the law contained in the Ten Commandments that Paul declares believers to be dead by the body of Christ, and to which he everywhere alludes as the rule of duty on which he and the other apostles found their exhortations to the churches. To this law he refers, when expressly quoting one of its commandments, in saying, "unless the law had said, 'You shall not covet'" (Rom. 7:7), he declares that it was ordained to life. According, then, to our Lord's answer to the lawyer regarding the law of the Decalogue, "This do and thou shalt live"; and His answer to the rich young man, "If thou wilt enter into life keep the commandments"; and to this declaration of the apostle to the same effect that the commandment was ordained to life, it is for the keeping of the Ten Commandments, which contain in substance the whole law of God, that the blessing of eternal life is to be awarded. Jesus declared that one jot or tittle of the law should not pass till all was fulfilled. He did fulfill it; and, being fulfilled by Him, it is fulfilled by all who are in Him, who is "the end of the law for righteousness to everyone who believes" (Rom. 10:4). If, then, any man shall ever "enter into life," he will enter it by having thus fulfilled the commandments without the exception of one jot or tittle belonging to any one of the ten.

Objections to the Permanent Obligation   43

It is these Ten Commandments, well nigh effaced from the heart of man, that were republished with such solemnity at Mount Sinai, written on the tables of stone, and deposited in the ark. These commandments were connected with the everlasting covenant given to Abraham and confirmed in Christ. They were proclaimed to Israel before the laws peculiar to that people were made, and they equally belong to all nations. It is these commandments, which it is the gracious promise of the new covenant shall be written by God in the hearts of His people.

> Behold, the days are coming, says the LORD, when I will make a new covenant with the house of Israel and with the house of Judah—not according to the covenant that I made with their fathers in the day that I took them by the hand to lead them out of the land of Egypt, My covenant which they broke, though I was a husband to them, says the LORD. But this *is* the covenant that I will make with the house of Israel after those days, says the LORD: I will put My law in their minds, and write it on their hearts; and I will be their God, and they shall be My people. (Jer. 31:31–33)

Now, this is not a fact respecting those statutes and judgments peculiar to Israel which are not thus written, but regarding only the moral law of the commandments, and all that results from it. And to this writing of the commandments of the two tables of the law on the hearts of

God's people the apostle particularly refers in the third chapter of the second epistle to the Corinthians, where he says, "Clearly you are an epistle of Christ, ministered by us, written not with ink but by the Spirit of the living God, not on tablets of stone but on tablets of flesh, that is, of the heart." By this allusion, we learn that the commandments, which had been written on the two tables of stone, are now written on the heart of every Christian. And what Christian is there who does not thank God that He has appointed for him the Sabbath day as a day of rest? And who does not feel the benefit of it when he is enabled to sanctify it as he ought?

–8–

The Observance of the Sabbath under the Christian Dispensation Is Fully Recognized by the Prophets

In the prophecies referring to the times of the gospel, the observance of a weekly Sabbath, so far from being classed among those shadowy ordinances that were to be abolished, is spoken of as a duty highly acceptable to God. The prophet Isaiah, although he had said nothing respecting the observance of the Sabbath when denouncing threatenings against the Jews, and exhorting them to obedience, beautifully enlarges on it when he comes to speak of the kingdom of the Messiah. After predicting, in the forty-ninth and following chapters, the establishment of that kingdom and the calling of the Gentiles, he proclaims, in the beginning of the fifty-sixth chapter, that the righteousness of God, which he there and in so many other places connects with salvation, was near to be revealed.

> Thus says the LORD:
> "Keep justice, and do righteousness,
> For My salvation is about to come,
> And My righteousness to be revealed.

> Blessed is the man who does this,
> And the son of man who lays hold on it;
> Who keeps from defiling the Sabbath,
> And keeps his hand from doing any evil."

Immediately after which, speaking both of the Gentiles and the eunuchs, when the distinction respecting the former and the exclusion of the latter from the congregation of the Lord should by the gospel be abolished, the prophet adds,

> Do not let the son of the foreigner
> Who has joined himself to the Lord
> Speak, saying,
> "The Lord has utterly separated me from
>   His people";
> Nor let the eunuch say,
> "Here I am, a dry tree."
> For thus says the Lord:
> "To the eunuchs who keep My Sabbaths,
> And choose what pleases Me,
> And hold fast My covenant,
> Even to them I will give in My house
> And within My walls a place and a name
> Better than that of sons and daughters;
> I will give them an everlasting name
> That shall not be cut off.
>
> "Also the sons of the foreigner
> Who join themselves to the Lord, to serve Him,
> And to love the name of the Lord, to be His
>   servants—

Recognized by the Prophets

Everyone who keeps from defiling the Sabbath,
And holds fast My covenant—
Even them I will bring to My holy mountain,
And make them joyful in My house of prayer.
Their burnt offerings and their sacrifices
Will be accepted on My altar;
For My house shall be called a house of prayer
   for all nations."

In the above passages, the importance of keeping the Sabbath is introduced no fewer than three times, and in relation to each of the three characters there specified. And while, on the one hand, polluting it is conjoined with doing evil, on the other, its observance is connected with doing judgment and justice—all that we owe to God and our neighbor—with giving ourselves to the Lord, loving His name, and being His servants. It is also connected with taking hold of His covenant—the covenant of peace spoken of (Isa. 54:10; Ezek. 34:25), that is, the gospel—and with receiving the Gentiles into that covenant, of whom it is said,

The Lord GOD, who gathers the outcasts of
   Israel, says,
"Yet I will gather to him
Others besides those who are gathered to him."
   (Isa. 56:8)

The duty then of observing the Sabbath, and the blessings connected with it, is here represented as belonging to that period when the name of God shall be great among the Gentiles; when Christ shall be God's salvation unto the ends of the earth (Isa. 49:6), predicted to be near to come; when His righteousness shall be revealed—namely, in the gospel (Rom. 1:17; 3:21); when the eunuchs and the sons of the stranger shall come to God's holy mountain; when His house shall be called a house of prayer for all people, in which they shall be joyful; and when their burnt offerings and their sacrifices shall be accepted upon His altar. In this and in similar passages, the prophets, in speaking of the times of the gospel, employ expressions relating to the services of that dispensation, during the continuance of which they wrote.

At the conclusion of his book of prophecy, in the end of the sixty-sixth chapter, where Isaiah once more declares the bringing in of the Gentiles and the introduction of the gospel dispensation, he again announces the perpetuity and never-ceasing solemnization of the Sabbath. "Thus says the LORD, 'Behold, I will extend peace to her [to Zion] like a river, and the glory of the Gentiles like a flowing stream'" (v. 12); "I will gather all nations and tongues; and they shall come and see My glory" (v. 18); "'For as the new heavens and the new earth which I will make shall remain before Me,' says the LORD, 'So shall your descendants and your name remain. And it shall come to pass that from one New Moon to another, and from one Sabbath to another, all flesh shall come to worship before Me,' says the LORD"

(vv. 22–23). In that period, then, during the reign of the Messiah, whose name shall "continue as long as the sun" and "shall endure forever," the observance of the Sabbath shall be as constant and as regular as the revolutions of the moon in the heavens.

By the importance thus attached to the keeping of the Sabbath, so often brought into view, and so intimately connected with the service of God, we learn that, under the Christian dispensation, and as forming a part of that law which is holy and just and good, the least commandment of which we are warned not to break or to teach others to do so, the Sabbath was to be considered as the grand support of the worship and service of God. This is particularly marked in the fifty-eighth chapter of Isaiah, where the prophet, after exposing the hypocrisy of the Jews, urges them to act in a manner that would be acceptable to God, and then proceeds to enlarge on the duty of sanctifying the Sabbath. Far from referring to it as a part of that yoke which was too heavy to be borne, or the handwriting of an ordinance that was to be blotted out, or taken out of the way, he represents it as God's "holy day, a delight, the holy of the Lord, honorable," on which His people, when they observed it as He commands, should find their delight in the Lord and should be highly rewarded by Him. Can an institution like this, characterized in this manner by Jehovah, to the observance of which He annexes His choicest blessings, be classed among the shadows that were to be abolished—with the sacrifices, and offerings, and burnt offerings for sin, in which God declared that He had no pleasure, and with the meats, and drinks, and divers washings, and carnal ordinances, imposed until the time of reformation, all forever to be done away with that covenant which made nothing perfect?

We have thus accumulated and demonstrated proof that the institution of the weekly Sabbath, announced at the beginning and embodied in the Decalogue, has ever been and continues to be equally binding with all the other parts of the law of everlasting obligation. In that law, the fourth commandment occupies a very distinguished place, essentially contributing to obedience to all the rest, while no other commandment has been so frequently enforced in the Scriptures. It is the only one of the ten in which the duty it enjoins is expressed both positively, "Keep it holy," and negatively, "In it thou shalt not do any work," all the other commandments being either solely prohibitory or solely preceptive. It is the only one of them all whose original institution is declared in Scripture.

The Change from the Last to the First Day of the Week Has Not Invalidated the Obligation of the Sabbath

Having now proved that the duty of the sanctification of the Sabbath has nothing in it peculiar to the law of Moses, or to any former dispensation, it remains to be shown that the change from the last to the first day of the week has neither made void the primary institution nor the fourth commandment, whose binding and permanent authority, enjoining the consecration of a seventh part of our time to God, continues unalterably the same.

"The Sabbath," said our Lord, "was made for man." It was made for his good, a day of rest from worldly business; for the special acknowledgment of God; and for the enjoyment of peculiar communion with Him. If the Sabbath was made for man, it was not a Jewish burden. It was for the good of man, not merely for the Jew. Yet He who is the Lord of the Sabbath may change the day of its observance. This, in fact, He has done; and in this passage there is not an obscure intimation of such a purpose. Of this change, as everything belonging to the new dispensation was shadowed forth under the old, we find, in the Old Testament, various typical and significant notices.

The heavens declare the glory of God, and when the foundations of the earth were laid, and the cornerstone thereof, the morning stars sang together, and all the sons of God shouted for joy. But God hath magnified His word above all His name, and a still more glorious display of His character and perfections has been given in the work of redemption than in that of the first creation. In the sixty-fifth chapter of Isaiah, where the prophet is referring to the kingdom of Christ, and the New Testament dispensation, that work is spoken of in the seventeenth verse as the creation of new heavens and a new earth, when Jerusalem—the church of God—should be a cause of rejoicing and when in comparison with that new creation, the glory of the former should not be remembered.

> Behold, I create new heavens and a new earth;
> And the former shall not be remembered or
>   come to mind.
> But be glad and rejoice forever in what I create;
> For behold, I create Jerusalem as a rejoicing,
> And her people a joy.

That God purposed to appoint the day of His resting from the work of this new creation as the Sabbath which He was afterward to bless and hallow in remembrance of it, in place of that day which He had formerly consecrated to the memory of His resting from the first creation, appears from His commanding the Israelites to observe the Sabbath in remembrance of their deliverance from Egyptian bondage. That deliverance was an eminent type of the redemption of His people by Christ from the bondage of Satan. But if the Israelites were commanded, in commemoration of this shadow, to sanctify one day in the week, which is the reason given for their doing so in the recapitulation of the fourth commandment (Deut. 5:15) instead of that formerly given to them at its first announcement respecting the creation (Gen. 2:2; Ex. 20:11), this was an intimation that the great and glorious work of which that deliverance was a shadow was afterward to be the object of weekly commemoration. "'Observe the Sabbath day, to keep it holy, as the LORD your God commanded you.... And remember that you were a slave in the land of Egypt, and the LORD your God brought you out from there by a mighty hand and by an outstretched arm; therefore the LORD your God commanded you to keep the Sabbath day.'"

The 118th psalm (vv. 19–24) clearly indicates the day in which the servants of God are by His appointment to enter into His sanctuary, to offer to Him praise, and to rejoice in commemoration of the resurrection of their Lord from the dead.

> Open to me the gates of righteousness;
> I will go through them,

> And I will praise the Lord.
> This is the gate of the Lord,
> Through which the righteous shall enter.
>
> I will praise You,
> For You have answered me,
> And have become my salvation.
>
> The stone which the builders rejected
> Has become the chief cornerstone.
> This was the Lord's doing;
> It is marvelous in our eyes.
> This is the day the Lord has made;
> We will rejoice and be glad in it.

These words are prophetical, and the twenty-second and twenty-third verses are again and again quoted in the New Testament and applied by the Lord Jesus to Himself. When He lay in the grave, He was as a stone which the builders had rejected, but when He arose from the dead, having vanquished all His enemies, He became the head stone of the spiritual temple of which His members are living stones (1 Peter 2:4–8). At the period of the old creation, God "rested on the seventh day from all His work which He had done," and all "the sons of God shouted for joy." In the same way, at the finishing of the new creation, the sons of God are here said to rejoice. This the disciples did at the resurrection of our Lord, as His people have done on that day ever since. That day, therefore, in which He rested from His work, they are to regard as "the day which the Lord hath made," properly and emphatically "the Lord's Day."

The change of the day of weekly rest, from the last to the first day of the week (that is, from the seventh to the eighth day), is indicated in various places throughout the Old Testament Scriptures. The work of creation was finished in six days, and on the seventh day God rested from His work, which completed a week, or the first series of time. The eighth day, then, was the first of a new series, and on this, the day of His resurrection, the Lord Jesus rested from the work of the new creation. The eighth day is accordingly signalized in the Old Testament, pointing in a manner most expressly to the day when Jesus entered into His rest and when in commemoration thereof His people are to rest. Of this the following are examples:

Circumcision was to be administered to children on the eighth day (Gen. 17:12), and till the eighth day the mother was ceremonially unclean (Lev. 12:2–3). Circumcision was the token of the covenant which God made with Abraham. "And he received the sign of circumcision, a seal of the righteousness of the faith which he had while still uncircumcised" (Rom. 4:11). Circumcision was not a seal of Abraham's faith or that he possessed righteousness or was justified, as it is almost constantly explained. It was a seal, pledge, or assurance of the reality of that righteousness which is received by the faith which Abraham had, in virtue of which, though not then existing, except in the purpose of God, he was justified, and that it should in its appointed time be introduced. This was the "everlasting righteousness," even the righteousness of God on account of which the gospel is the power of God unto salvation to everyone that believeth. Circumcision, then, being such a seal to Abraham, from whom Christ was to spring, was to be impressed on himself and his posterity and to be performed on the eighth day, the day on which that righteousness was, by the resurrection of the Messiah, to be "brought in." As soon as the pledge was thus redeemed, the rite of circumcision ceased. At that early period, then, we find a clear indication of the high distinction which, in a distant age, was to be conferred on the eighth day. The same intimation strikingly pervades the Jewish dispensation in its various typical and shadowy institutions.

Until the eighth day of their age, the firstborn of cattle, which belonged to the Lord, were not offered or received by Him. "On the eighth day you shall give it to Me" (Ex. 22:30). On the eighth day, but not before, animals were accepted in sacrifice. "When a bull or a sheep or a goat is born, it shall be seven days with its mother; and from the eighth day and thereafter it shall be accepted as an offering made by fire to the LORD" (Lev. 22:27).

On the eighth day the consecration of Aaron, as high priest, and his sons, after various ceremonies, was completed (Lev. 9:1). On the eighth day the cleansing

The Change from the Last to the First Day 57

of the leprosy, which was typical of cleansing from sin, took place (Lev. 14:10). On the eighth day the cleansing from issues, emblematical also of sin, was effected (Lev. 15:14, 29). On the eighth day atonement was made for the Nazirite who was defiled (Num. 6:10).

The eighth day corresponds with the first day of the week, on which, according to all these typical appointments, the following occurred: Jesus was received as the firstborn from the dead; His sacrifice was accepted, and on which, as the Great High Priest, He was "consecrated forevermore" and when He made atonement for His people, by which they are cleansed from sin.

The eighth day was sanctified when the dedication of the temple—that illustrious type of the body of the Redeemer—was completed and the ark of the covenant placed in it. "Solomon kept the feast seven days, and all Israel with him, a very great assembly from the entrance of Hamath to the Brook of Egypt. And on the eighth day they held a sacred assembly" (2 Chron. 7:8–9)—on that day, when the Lord was afterward to create upon every dwelling place of Mount Zion, and upon her assemblies, a cloud and smoke by day and the shining of a flaming fire by night.

In sanctifying the temple, in the time of Hezekiah, "they began to sanctify on the first day of the first month, and on the eighth day of the month they came to the vestibule of the LORD. So they sanctified the house of the LORD in eight days, and on the sixteenth day of the first month they finished," when the whole was terminated by the offering of sacrifice and the solemn worship of God (2 Chron. 29:17, 20).

Ezekiel, in his vision of the city and temple, which appears to give figuratively, and in Old Testament language, a description of the Redeemer's kingdom and church, says, "'Seven days they shall make atonement for the altar and purify it, and so consecrate it. When these days are over it shall be, on the eighth day and thereafter, that the priests shall offer your burnt offerings and your peace offerings on the altar; and I will accept you,' says the Lord GOD" (43:26–27).

The feast of tabernacles was to be celebrated on the *fifteenth*, which corresponds with the eighth day.

> Speak to the children of Israel, saying: "The fifteenth day of this seventh month shall be the Feast of Tabernacles for seven days to the LORD. On the first day there shall be a holy convocation. You shall do no customary work on it. For seven days you shall offer an offering made by fire to the LORD. On the eighth day you shall have a holy convocation, and you shall offer an offering made by fire to the LORD. It is a sacred assembly, and you shall do no customary work on it....
>
> Also on the fifteenth day of the seventh month, when you have gathered in the fruit of the land, you shall keep the feast of the LORD for seven days; on the first day there shall be a sabbath-rest, and on the eighth day a sabbath-rest." (Lev. 23:34–36, 39)

The Change from the Last to the First Day

The feast of tabernacles, which thus terminated on the eighth day, furnishes a remarkable representation of the vanishing of the legal sacrifices when their consummation took place by the offering of the one sacrifice. On the first day of this feast, thirteen bullocks, two rams, and fourteen lambs were offered. On the following six days, the number of bullocks was decreased by one each day, so that, on the seventh day, only seven were offered, and two rams and fourteen lambs. But on the eighth day, the number was reduced to one bullock, when these sacrifices were ended. "On the eighth day you shall have a sacred assembly. You shall do no customary work. You shall present a burnt offering, an offering made by fire as a sweet aroma to the LORD: one bull, one ram, seven lambs in their first year without blemish" (Num. 29:35–36). Thus the offering of only one bullock, one ram, and seven lambs (the number denoting perfection) on the eighth day, although many had been offered on the preceding days but gradually diminishing in number, was strikingly emblematical of the one offering by which Jesus Christ, on the eighth day, the first day of the week, made an end of sins and by one offering perfected forever them that are sanctified. At this feast, in the time of Ezra, when he read the book of the law to the people, a solemn assembly was held on the eighth day. "Also day by day, from the first day until the last day, he read from the Book of the Law of God. And they kept the feast seven days; and on the eighth day there was a sacred assembly, according to the prescribed manner" (Neh. 8:18; viz., the manner prescribed, Lev. 23:39).

When the sheaf of the firstfruits was to be brought to the priest, it was to be accepted on the eighth day: "He shall wave the sheaf before the LORD, to be accepted on your behalf; on the day after the Sabbath the priest shall wave it. And you shall offer on that day, when you wave the sheaf, a male lamb of the first year, without blemish, as a burnt offering to the LORD" (Lev. 23:11–12). This was a distinguished type of the resurrection of Him who was "the first fruits of them that slept," who arose from the dead on the morrow after the Sabbath—that is, the eighth day, or the first day of the week.

Not only was the eighth day signalized in so remarkable a manner, in connection with various typical appointments, the fiftieth day—the first day after seven times seven days, or seven weeks, corresponding with the eighth day after seven days, and both with the first day of the week—was in like manner distinguished.

At the reaping and gathering in of the harvest, two wave loaves were to be presented on the fiftieth day after presenting the sheaf of the firstfruits.

> And you shall count for yourselves from the day after the Sabbath, from the day that you brought the sheaf of the wave offering: seven Sabbaths shall be completed. Count fifty days to the day after the seventh Sabbath; then you shall offer a

new grain offering to the LORD. You shall bring from your dwellings two wave loaves of two-tenths of an ephah. They shall be of fine flour; they shall be baked with leaven. They are the firstfruits to the LORD.... And you shall proclaim on the same day that it is a holy convocation to you. You shall do no customary work on it. (Lev. 23:15–17, 21)

The year of Jubilee was the fiftieth year, and not the forty-ninth, which was the last of the sabbatical years. "And you shall count seven sabbaths of years for yourself, seven times seven years; and the time of the seven sabbaths of years shall be to you forty-nine years.... And you shall consecrate the fiftieth year, and proclaim liberty throughout all the land to all its inhabitants. It shall be a Jubilee for you; and each of you shall return to his possession" (Lev. 25:8, 10). This fiftieth year, the first year after the sabbatical year of seven weeks, corresponds with the eighth day, the first day of the week.

Can it be supposed that the eighth day, thus signalized from so early a period, before the legal dispensation, and in so many ways during its continuance, and by one of the latest of the prophets, comprising in all more than thirteen hundred years—can it be imagined that the eighth, the fifteenth, and the fiftieth day, all of the same import, were thus distinguished without a special purpose, and that in the wisdom of God they were not expressly specified for some very important end? Connected as they were with the most solemn services of

God's ancient people, and in a manner so conspicuous with the most remarkable typical observances, they held forth a striking notification of the future change from that day which had been appointed to commemorate God's resting from the work of creation to the day on which the Son of God rested from the work of redemption. This purpose is fully developed in the New Testament, where He who is the Lord of the Sabbath—without in the smallest degree impairing, relaxing, or changing the obligation to observe a seventh day's rest—appropriated to Himself the eighth day, the first instead of the last day of the week, and by recording His name upon it, calling it the Lord's Day, has blessed and sanctified it for the use of His people. It may here be remarked that by the early Christians the Sabbath was also denominated the eighth day. Barnabas, the companion of the apostle Paul, calls this the eighth day, in distinction from the seventh day Sabbath, which he says "is the beginning of another world; and therefore, we keep the eighth day joyfully, in which Jesus rose from the dead, and being manifested ascended into heaven." It was known, too, by the fathers, by the name of the eighth day, as by Ignatius, Irenaeus, Origen, and others. "Every eighth day," says Tertullian, "is the Christian's festival."

The duty of sanctifying the first day of the week is taught in the New Testament not by direct precept but in the way of approved example or reference in which several other institutions are there enjoined. Instruction

The Change from the Last to the First Day

as to anything further respecting the duty, or the manner of discharging it besides the change from the last to the first day of the week, was unnecessary, since all things else remain the same as formerly and are so solemnly enjoined and enforced in the Old Testament. Nothing more than this fact of the change of the day needed afterward to be made known. This change we learn, first, by the honor conferred on that day by the Lord, in repeatedly appearing on it to His disciples after His resurrection; second, by the outpouring of the Holy Ghost on the day of Pentecost; third, by the practice of the apostles, to whom the keys of the kingdom were delivered, and also by that of the first churches under their immediate guidance; and, finally, we are taught this change by the distinctive appellation it received, of "The Lord's Day," when our Lord appeared to His disciple John.

On the first day of the week, being the day on which the Lord rose from the dead and rested from the work of the new creation, He appeared at different times to His disciples. "Then, the same day at evening, being the first day of the week, when the doors were shut where the disciples were assembled, for fear of the Jews, Jesus came and stood in the midst" (John 20:19). It is here proper to remark that the literal translation of the original, rendered the first day of the week, is the first of the Sabbaths. The rendering, however, in this place is proper, as well as in other places in the New Testament where the same phrase occurs—as Matthew 28:1;

Mark 16:2, 9; Luke 24:1; John 20:1, 19; Acts 20:7; and 1 Corinthians 16:2—since the word in the original for Sabbath also signifies week.

On the same day, in the following week, when the disciples were again assembled, Jesus appeared in the midst of them: "And after eight days His disciples were again inside, and Thomas with them. Jesus came, the doors being shut, and stood in the midst, and said, 'Peace to you!'" (John 20:26).

The day of Pentecost, which signifies the fiftieth day, was eminently honored. It was the first day of the week, the day of the outpouring of the Holy Ghost in His abundant and miraculous gifts, the day of the promulgation of the gospel in the presence of men from all nations and of the conversion of "about three thousand souls." Here we have the explanation of the mystery in the Old Testament of the fiftieth day, connected, as we have seen, with remarkable events and ordinances. On the fiftieth day after the departure from Egypt, the law was delivered from Mount Sinai, which, corresponding with the first day of the week, was 1,500 years afterward fulfilled on that day. That law was delivered, accompanied with thunderings and lightnings, and now, on the corresponding day, came a sound from heaven "as of a rushing mighty wind," and "divided tongues, as of fire" sat upon each of the disciples. The day of Pentecost, too, was the fiftieth day from the resurrection of Jesus Christ, when He "became the first fruits of them that slept" and the day of the first fruits of the Christian church. The fiftieth year of jubilee, when every man returned into his own possession which he had sold or forfeited, also corresponded with that fiftieth day, the day of Pentecost, on which so remarkable a proof was given that the price of the redemption of Christ's people had been paid, and that for them He had entered into the possession of His and their eternal inheritance. The giving of the Holy Ghost—the coming of the promised Comforter, being thus vouchsafed on the first day of the week, confirmed the newly instituted season, which was henceforth to be the Christian Sabbath. And on this day not merely the apostles but all the disciples (Acts 1:15; 2:1) were with one accord (as being the day of their stated meeting) in one place.

The first churches under the guidance of the apostles assembled on the first day of the week. The apostle Paul, and those who accompanied him, abode seven days at Troas. "Now on the first day of the week, when the disciples came together to break bread, Paul, ready to depart the next day, spoke to them" (Acts 20:7). Here we learn that it was their common custom to meet on this day for holding their religious assemblies and observing the stated ordinances of worship. The time appointed, too, to collect the contributions for the poor was the first day of the week. "Now concerning the collection for the saints, as I have given orders to the churches of Galatia, so you must do also: On the first day of the week let each one of you lay something aside, storing up as he may prosper, that there be no collections when I come" (1 Cor. 16:1–2). It was not, then, on account of anything peculiar to the church at Corinth that Paul commanded that this duty should be performed on the first day of the week, since he had enjoined the same on the distant churches of Galatia, and the apostle elsewhere declares that he taught the same things everywhere in all the churches (1 Cor. 4:17; 7:17).

The first day of the week was further distinguished and honored in a very remarkable manner by the Lord Himself—in His glorious appearance in the Isle of Patmos and by the prophetic vision which He vouchsafed to His servant John—of all that was to take place respecting His church to the end of time.

In the relation of this vision, the apostle, writing by the inspiration of the Holy Ghost, calls the day on which he was favored with it the Lord's Day. This term being here introduced without any remark or explanation must have been well understood by all who read and heard the words of this prophecy (Rev. 1:3)—that is, by all Christians as well as by the seven churches whom the apostle specially addressed. This establishes beyond contradiction that under the Christian dispensation there is a Lord's Day. All days are His. If, then, one of them is called the Lord's Day in distinction from the rest, it must be His day in a peculiar sense. It must be devoted to His honor. It must be His as the Lord's Supper is His. As, then, the Lord's Supper distinguishes and separates the holy communion of the bread and wine from an ordinary social meal, so the Lord's Day distinguishes and separates one day from the rest in the week. This was the day of His triumph over all the powers of darkness. It is the Lord's Day—not a part of a day, but a whole day, and not our day, but His day—in the same way as the Lord's Supper is His supper and not our supper. It should likewise be observed that the reason given in the fourth commandment for abstaining from work and for hallowing the seventh day is, "Six days you shall labor and do all your work, but the seventh day is the Sabbath of the LORD your God. In it you shall do no work." And, therefore, the same obligation must follow as to the "Lord's Day," because it is the day of the Lord. In the Lord's Supper, we have a symbolical representation of the death of Christ, and in the Lord's Day we have a commemoration of His resurrection every week.

If anyone hesitates to admit that the observance of the first day of the week is commanded in the New Testament because not enjoined by direct precept, he has not attended to the manner in which the various parts of our duty are there taught, and he should ask himself on what ground he observes the first day of the week. Is it because all Christians agree in doing so? In this there is nothing valid. The consent or practice of all the Christians and of all the churches on earth cannot add to, or take from, or change one iota of the law of God. What that law is must be learned from the Scriptures, either by direct precept or from the approved practice recorded in them of Christians or churches under the guidance of the apostles and thus stamped with their authority. To the apostles alone were the keys of the kingdom of heaven delivered by their divine Master, first to Peter (Matt. 16:19) and afterward to all the rest (18:18), who, in order that they might be His witnesses, had all seen Him after His resurrection; who all had "the signs of an Apostle"; who have no successors in office, and whose doctrine, being infallible, binds in heaven and on earth. Christians have nothing to do but to repeat and to obey the laws, in whatever manner enjoined by our Lord and His apostles. Why are churches formed? Why do they assemble on the first day of the week? Why are they to consist of persons only of a certain character? For none of these, and certain other things that are practiced by Christians, is there any direct precept. But all of them, of which we have approved example in the Word of God, are, notwithstanding, equally binding, as if in direct terms they had been commanded. To the practice of the first churches under his direction, and to his own practice, the apostle Paul appeals as of equal authority with his express injunctions. "If anyone seems to be contentious, we have no such custom, nor do the churches of God" (1 Cor. 11:16). The approved customs of the first churches were fixed by the apostles and are therefore equally binding as their commands; and their commands, as speaking by the Holy Ghost, are equally obligatory as those of the Lord. "He who hears you hears Me, he who rejects you rejects Me, and he who rejects Me rejects Him who sent Me" (Luke 10:16). By the words which He hath spoken, and those of His apostles, whose words bind and loose in heaven and on earth, all shall be judged at the last day. If any man shall add to these words or take from them, God shall take away his part out of the book of life.

Although the first day of the week was appointed to be observed as the Sabbath under the Christian dispensation, yet the observance of the last day, that had been sanctified from the beginning, was likewise permitted during the continuance of the Jewish state. This was analogous to allowing the temple service and the sacrifices, although rendered inefficacious by the offering of the one great sacrifice, to continue till the whole of them was put an end to by the destruction of Jerusalem. Giving unnecessary offense to the Jews was thus avoided, while an opportunity was furnished, during all that period, of preaching the gospel in the synagogues where they assembled every Sabbath day, of which the apostles regularly availed themselves. But in the book of Revelation, as we have now seen, written after the Jewish state and polity were finally overthrown, the first day of the week, as that which the Son of God had appropriated for His peculiar service, of which from the first sufficient intimation had been given, so that His disciples had observed it all along after His resurrection, was, in a manner still more marked, exclusively designated in His Word as the Lord's Day—the name by which it has been known and recognized by all Christians ever since.

The day of rest enjoined to be observed by Christians, although now transferred from the last to the first day of the week, or the eighth day from the creation, is still the seventh day, "after the six working days," as was the Sabbath of the first institution and of the fourth commandment. Thus, all the change is only a change of the beginning and the ending of the days of labor, the number of which continue as before. The words, therefore, of the fourth commandment, "Six days you shall labor and do all your work, but the seventh day is the Sabbath of the LORD your God. In it you shall do no work," form no objection to the Christian Sabbath, as if it changed or discontinued the duty enjoined in that commandment, since these words retain the same force as before. Neither can any objection be drawn from the words that follow: "For in six days the LORD made the heavens and the earth, the sea, and all that is in them, and rested the seventh day. Therefore the LORD blessed the Sabbath day and hallowed it." These words have not become insignificant by the establishment of the first-day Sabbath; they remain, as to their principal object, in full force. Their object was to present a motive to rest on the seventh day after laboring six days following; because of this God had given the example. And on this

The Change from the Last to the First Day

account, as well as from the examples of the sanctification of the first day of the week, Christians are to rest not on every eighth, or ninth, or tenth day but on every seventh day. God wrought six days and rested on the seventh day and called it the Sabbath, or rest of the Lord. Jesus, the Lord of the Sabbath, in like manner rested from the work of the new creation on the first day of the week and has now appropriated it as His day. And not only was it appointed to commemorate the great event of His resurrection, but as it is to be observed on one day in seven, it is so instituted as likewise to commemorate that first creation, when after the work of six days God rested on the seventh. Without reference to this no reason can be given why the resurrection should be celebrated once in seven days and not at any other fixed period. The fourth commandment, then, in everything essential, remains unchanged. In substance it continues precisely as before, commanding us to sanctify the seventh day; and the reason of enjoining this continues the same, with the difference only of God's having rested from the work of the new (as He formerly did from that of the old) creation, on which account man is still to rest on the seventh day, after six days of labor. It is a part of that law which cannot be broken. Strict obedience to it continues to be the duty of every Christian; and in order to understand its proper and spiritual import, the inspired commentary of the prophet Isaiah (58:13) on the obligation and observance of the Sabbath, referring to the times of the gospel, should be attentively considered. Some have scrupled to denominate the first day of the week the Sabbath day. But it should be remembered that this is the name by which it is so often designated in the New Testament, according to the literal rendering of the passage quoted in a previous page.

Conclusion

The Sabbath, instituted for man, both in a state of innocence and of sin, displays in a remarkable manner the goodness of God and forms a distinguished part of that law which is the law of love. It was appointed before the curse was pronounced that in the sweat of his face man should eat bread; yet after he had sinned, it was not abolished, but continued as a permanent mitigation of that sentence. The fourth commandment is not a burden, like those institutions that were peculiar to the Jews. They were a yoke (Acts 15:10), but this is a blessing. And man does not suffer by it, but is benefited. By our fall in Adam we became slaves to Satan, and God might have condemned us to labor all the days of the week. But He has given us a reprieve for one day. His providence so orders it that men in all conditions shall participate in the curse and eat the fruit of the earth in the sweat of their face. Is it not then a blessing when He gives us one day of rest? Had He required us to labor the whole seven days, there would not have been more food than there is now. There is not more in those countries where the Sabbath is not observed than where it is observed. Nor is any country benefited by its neglect. On the contrary, it would be political wisdom to give the full benefit of the Sabbath in every country to man and to beast. We see that if the Israelites did not gather the manna on the seventh day, they gathered as much on the day preceding as supplied them on the Sabbath; and in allowing, in the sabbatical year, the land to rest, it produced for them as much in the sixth as sufficed them both in that year and in the seventh.

This respite from toil ought, then, to be thankfully acknowledged as a high privilege bestowed on man, doomed to labor on account of sin. But the institution of the Sabbath confers on him a nobler privilege. It is set apart for our use, to be the means of calling our attention from interests merely temporal to those that are spiritual and eternal. It is a day appointed for special communion with God, and the bodily rest is chiefly to be prized as subservient to this end. Bodily rest is necessary on that day for its spiritual improvement; and its spiritual improvement is necessary in order that we may not abuse it by indulging in sloth and idleness, and thus exposing ourselves to the seductions of Satan. The Sabbath, then, is a day to be devoted to the service of the Lord and to our own spiritual edification in all those exercises connected with and contributing to these ends. It is a day of the greatest enjoyment that Christians have

Conclusion

on earth; and God, in its institution, has shown His love for His church. A great part of the vigor of the spiritual life, and of aptitude for the duty of growing in grace, and in the knowledge of our Lord and Savior Jesus Christ, depends on our sanctifying this day, as well as our enjoyment of the manifestations of His love, exciting our longing and ardent desires for a better (that is, a heavenly) country.

Thanks be to God for the institution of the Sabbath, of binding obligation in every period of the world since its creation, and on all men, although so often and so much neglected. In the Old Testament, we see by its being so frequently and solemnly enjoined—as well as by the gracious promises annexed to its observance, the fearful threatenings pronounced, and the punishments inflicted in case of its infraction—how great was the importance which God attached to the Sabbath. Nehemiah imputes all the calamities which befell the Jews to their profanation of that day, and represents this as one of the principal causes which had brought on them the wrath of God:

> In those days I saw people in Judah treading winepresses on the Sabbath, and bringing in sheaves, and loading donkeys with wine, grapes, figs, and all kinds of burdens, which they brought into Jerusalem on the Sabbath day. And I warned them about the day on which they were selling provisions. Men of Tyre dwelt there also, who brought in fish and all kinds of goods, and sold

them on the Sabbath to the children of Judah, and in Jerusalem.

Then I contended with the nobles of Judah, and said to them, "What evil thing is this that you do, by which you profane the Sabbath day? Did not your fathers do thus, and did not our God bring all this disaster on us and on this city? Yet you bring added wrath on Israel by profaning the Sabbath." (Neh. 13:15–18)

The observance of the sabbatical years having been neglected by the Jews, their captivity in Babylon endured seventy years, to "fulfill," it is said, "the word of the LORD by the mouth of Jeremiah, until the land had enjoyed her Sabbaths. As long as she lay desolate she kept Sabbath, to fulfill seventy years" (2 Chron. 36:21; Lev. 26:32, 43). In the prophecies of Jeremiah (chap. 17) we observe on the one hand the signal blessings annexed to the sanctification of the Sabbath, while on the other, the following awful threatenings in case of its desecration are subjoined. "But if you will not heed Me to hallow the Sabbath day, such as not carrying a burden when entering the gates of Jerusalem on the Sabbath day, then I will kindle a fire in its gates, and it shall devour the palaces of Jerusalem, and it shall not be quenched." We find, too, as stated in the preceding pages, that the observance of the holy Sabbath stands connected with and is the grand support of our obedience to all the other commandments, both of the first and second table of the law, which enjoin our duty to God and man.

Works of necessity that cannot be done on the day before, nor left undone till the day following, as well as works of mercy, are permitted on the Sabbath. But for a man on that day to employ himself in his ordinary labors, to speak of them, or even to allow them to occupy his thoughts is to oppose the beneficent purpose of the Lawgiver in appointing it and to contemn His authority; and if the business of the world (which on other days of the week is not only permitted but enjoined as a duty) be on this day criminal, how much must it be profaned by those frivolous amusements and recreations which are often resorted to on this sacred day, or by spending it in sloth and idleness. "He that sinneth against me wrongeth his own soul."

The day of rest is a weekly and solemn recognition of the authority of God. It ought to be employed in religious exercises, both public and private, for which it is set apart; and these exercises should be accounted the repose and refreshment of the soul. That which should occupy us on the Sabbath is the grand concern of our life. To serve and honor God is the end for which we were created; and with joy we should dedicate the seventh part of our time to His immediate and uninterrupted service, and so rest on "the Sabbath day, according to the commandment."

As the day of rest is peculiarly destined to religious services, so it is the day in which they who seek God may expect His peculiar benediction and the divine communications of His grace. The ordinances of God are the means of grace, and in the observance of these ordinances He has promised His special blessing. This is the Lord's Day which bears His name, and He has said, "In every place where I record My name I will come to you, and I will bless you." If on this day God has specially commanded us to seek Him, we may with confidence conclude that in a special manner on this day He will be found of us. The purpose of God to vouchsafe His blessings to those who observe the day of rest is included in the declaration that "the LORD blessed the Sabbath day and hallowed it." Not only, then, hath He sanctified that day, but He has blessed it. God has from the beginning given it His blessing, which He will bestow on all who consecrate it to His service. But if on account of finishing the work of the creation of the world the seventh day was blessed, how much more is it blessed because of the completion of the work of redemption? On that day the Lord Jesus ceased from His work and entered into His rest. It was the day on which He was delivered from the chains of death, when He was declared to be the Son of God, in which the promises to Him of His Father were accomplished and all power was given to Him in heaven and on earth. How much, then, may God be expected to honor this day and to bless His people in the observance of it with all spiritual blessings in Christ Jesus our Lord.

The Sabbath, then, the day of rest, the forerunner of the eternal rest, ought to be gratefully recognized and fondly cherished; and the manner in which it should be observed is fully declared in the Scriptures. The prophet Isaiah (58:13–14), referring to gospel times and instructing the servants of God to act so that their light may break forth as the morning, and their righteousness go before them, and the glory of the Lord be their reward, adds,

> If you turn away your foot from the Sabbath,
> From doing your pleasure on My holy day,
> And call the Sabbath a delight,
> The holy day of the LORD honorable,
> And shall honor Him, not doing your own ways,
> Nor finding your own pleasure,
> Nor speaking your own words,
> Then you shall delight yourself in the LORD;
> And I will cause you to ride on the high hills of
>   the earth,
> And feed you with the heritage of Jacob your
>   father.
> The mouth of the Lord has spoken.

The Sabbath is a day which beautifully sets forth the long-suffering, goodness, and enduring mercy of Jehovah. Most of the divine institutions under the law, and some of the ordinances of the gospel, are peculiarly intended to bring to our remembrance the guilt or the consequences of sin. The Sabbath, on the contrary, traces its origin to a time when man walked in innocence and to a place which was hallowed by the immediate presence of the Lord. The children of Israel were not commanded to observe a day which neither they nor their fathers had known, but rather to "remember" an institution which they had forgotten in the cruel bondage of Egypt, and to keep holy a day which their God still continued to claim as His inalienable property. Jesus Christ came not to destroy but to fulfill the law and the prophets; and having Himself declared the Sabbath to be His own, so by His inspired apostles He has left the impress of His name upon one day of seven.

Amid the joys of Eden man delighted to walk with God and hailed the privilege of communion with his Creator. Amid the cares and trials of a troubled and sinful world, the Christian, too, delights to hallow the Lord's Day and thus to participate in its present benefits and its emblematic happiness. He sees in it the loving kindness of his Lord, at once providing for him a retreat from labor and a fountain at which to refresh his weary soul. He feels it to be in itself a comfort, and in its enjoyment he decries by faith the rest which remains to the people of God.